Office 365

What's new?

Ina Koys

Short & Spicy, Vol. 3

Contents

- 0   What we're going to talk about 1
- 1   Generally 2
  - 1.1   Visual innovations 2
  - 1.2   Storages with different benefits 6
  - 1.3   Sharing files 11
  - 1.4   New and improved general features 16
  - 1.5   New entries in the Insert tab 22
  - 1.6   Draw Tab 25
  - 1.7   Picture Format tab 28
  - 1.8   Help and support 29
  - 1.9   Backstage area 31
- 2   Word 35
- 3   Excel 41
- 4   PowerPoint 60
- 5   Outlook 74
  - 5.1   View and backstage settings 74
  - 5.2   E-Mail 79
  - 5.3   Calendar 85
  - 5.4   Groups 87
  - 5.5   Insights and MyAnalytics 92
- 6   More 94

0   What we're going to talk about

'**Office 365**' was Microsoft's initial naming for a comprehensive package of applications and servers. Later, it was re-named to '**Microsoft 365**'. It's rented from Microsoft directly or via a service partner and normally runs from the respective servers.

Regarding the 'normal' Office applications run from there, they were for long identical with the Office packages of the time. Now, Microsoft turned away from this practise. They are now rolling out any changes and improvements as soon as they feel they're finished. Therefore, also this little book will continuously get changed along with the Office applications. Still, different update stages will occur and are normal.

Here, we will only talk about the classic Office applications like Word, Excel, PowerPoint, and Outlook. The other apps – more or less intensively used – will maybe later find room in a different booklet.

1 Generally

As mentioned above: Office 365 is no static product. It develops and changes and maybe looks different on your screen as we are getting the changes on a different time scale. Microsoft activates new features as soon as they are finished, but it may take weeks or months until they reach each and every customer. Private accounts and small companies will often get them instantly, in larger companies the IT department will have to check the changes before rolling them out for every workplace.

Indeed, there is by now a whole lot of new features compared with Office 2016 and 2019, even though one may have to have a second look sometimes.

Let's begin with something that experienced a kind of split: OneNote. It used to belong to the Office package and then became part of Windows 10. In Windows it was slightly modified and cooperates with Outlook only in a very basic way. Maybe therefore, Microsoft heard the voice of the customers and now offers the former Office-OneNote for free download. For a look into the respective features, my booklet 'The Digital Notebook' is available.

1.1 Visual innovations

For a couple of versions, the interface philosophy of Microsoft Office apps did not change much anymore. Still, clarity and conciseness did sometimes. Anyway, if you like the Dark Mode of Windows, you can now link it to the Office applications via **File / Options**.

Generally

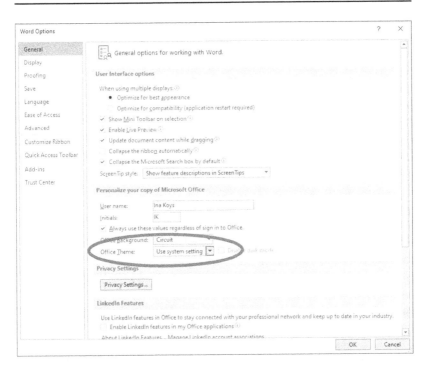

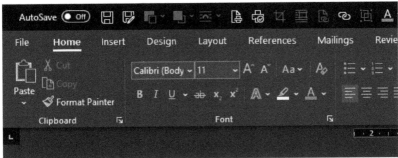

Regardless of the colour theme, one still can imagine the buttons as arranged on tabs. But as they are getting more and more discreet and abstractly displayed, one sometimes has a hard time to figure it out.

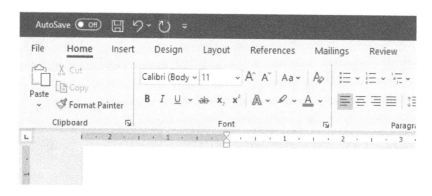

Only a faint marking under **Home** still lets us know we are in the **Home** tab. Also please notice the nostalgic **Save** symbol. One needs to work with the computer since pretty long to figure out it's meant to be a floppy disk – and what the heck a floppy disk used to be for.

On an absolutely blank machine with no previously installed Office, the tabs are now sometimes hidden in total. A double click on any of the tab titles brings the tabs back – as it used to be since they were invented.

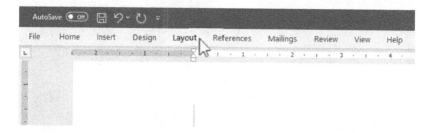

But let's take a closer look at the tabs. The common and frequently used features will certainly quickly get found again. But even more than 10 years after their invention still not everyone understood and internalized the concept of context-sensitive tabs. These tabs are only displayed along with their corresponding elements, i.e., with pictures. Only if one already inserted and clicked a picture the **Picture Format** tab is displayed.

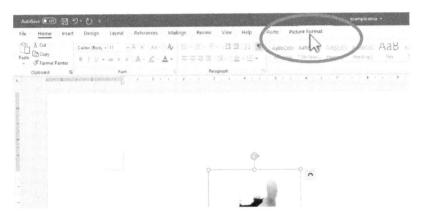

But it's hard to figure out meanwhile that the tab is not active at the moment and needs to be clicked in order to be brought forward and used. One simply needs to get have a second look and get used to it, then it'll work.

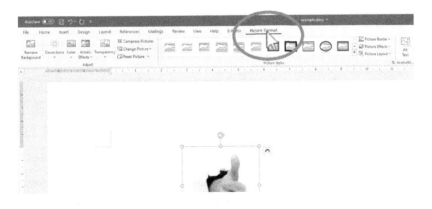

1.2 Storages with different benefits

New in Office 365 is a philosophy that impacts the work interface and the long-time unchanged habits of working on the computer as well. If one now i.e., intends to save a document, the dialogue suggests saving on OneDrive:

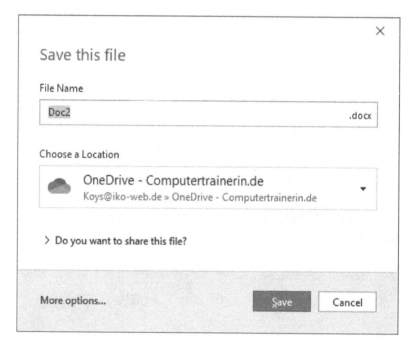

This cloud storage comes with every Office 365 license. It is safe in any meaning of the word and maybe the most important reason why there's a big rush of companies into the cloud.

First, let's have a look at what happens if you follow the suggestion. Clicking the little arrow one can browse the recently used folders. Using the three dots one also can specify a standard storage.

Generally

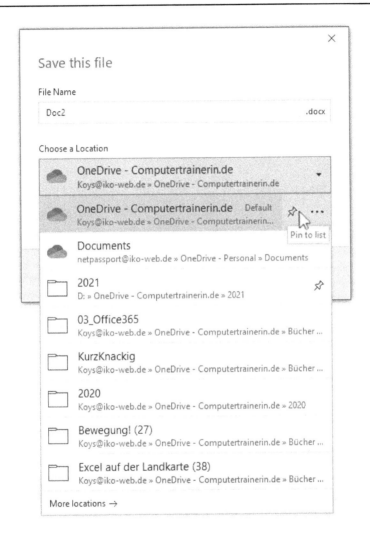

After selecting and clicking a folder, the document reports its saving status.

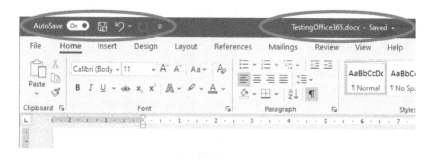

But something else happens, too. The **AutoSave** symbol in the title bar is active now. From now on, one does not need to remember saving the file anymore. For any file stored on the OneDrive, it's getting done automatically in the background without user activity. If there is no current internet connection, the file is stored temporarily on the local hard disk and silently synchronized next time you connect to the cloud.

But what if you change your mind while working with a file and want to undo some of your last already saved steps? That will still work via the **Undo** symbol in the quick access toolbar just right of the floppy disk symbol. And if you'd like to restore an elder version, also this is now done easily. All versions are kept in the cloud and can be recalled using the arrow next the file name.

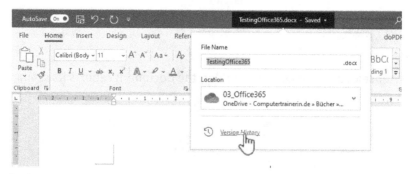

Now previous versions can be displayed and via mouse click restored as current version or saved as a new file.

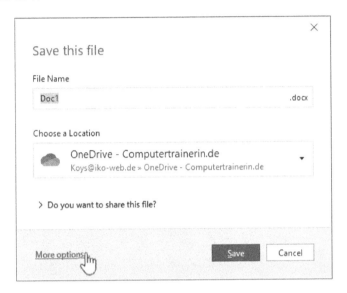

But of course, one does not need to store the files in the cloud. A click on **More options** leads you into the well-known **Save As** dialogue for all possible drives and folders.

Here, you also have the option to pin frequently used folders to the top of the list. Simply click the pin symbol and you'll never need to search for that folder again. If you are you still looking for a certain directory, go to **Browse**.

After that, you can pick any storing place as you like. Still, keep in mind that on local drives the **AutoSave** does not work. Here, you need to remember saving files as you did before.

Cloud drives are a good and reliable storage place for your files. But if you don't want to use it, you can determine in *File / Options / Save* to be first directed to a local drive.

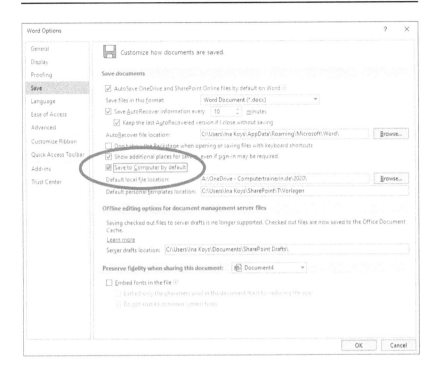

1.3 Sharing files

Really exciting about working in cloud drives is the possibility to work simultaneously with others on the same file. By default, this feature is activated for everyone. Still, the administrator can restrict the access and only allow co-operation within the same company. You may want to check this using your private email.

You can share a file in different ways. The easiest one is right in the **Save this file** window.

Generally

Here, you can make your decision what kind of access you grant. By default, the recipient can edit. If you only want to provide reading permission, it can be adjusted under the pen symbol. After clicking **Save**, the recipient simultaneously gets a standard email and the granted access on the server, too. One does not need to click anything in the mail or even notice it to exercise the permissions.

If that doesn't meet all your intensions, you have a separate **Share** button in the top right corner of your app window.

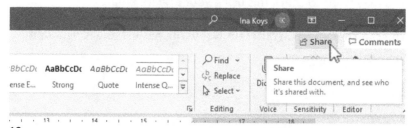

Here, you have more detailed options like expiration of rights or the permission to download a file.

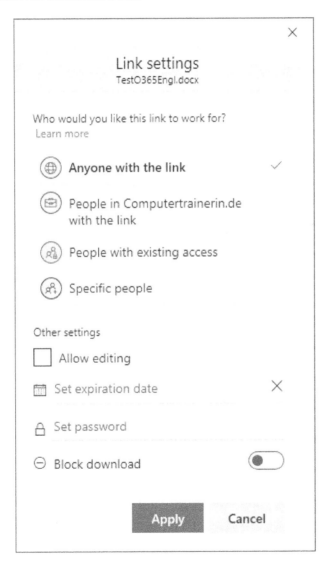

If you picked and adjusted the appropriate permissions, you only need to supply the email of the recipient. The server may replace the email with a known username.

Now, again, two things will happen the same time: The permissions are stored on the server and the recipient receives an email with the notification without you bothering.

Also, consider the difference between permission for a certain person, and sending a link that could be forwarded to anyone. Both ways, if set incorrectly, may lead to undesirable consequences.

If you later intend to review and maybe fix granted permissions, the way to get it done is not that obvious. But of course it exists: check out the three dots in the share dialogue.

In the now opening **Manage Access** window you can review, apply and adjust any desired changes.

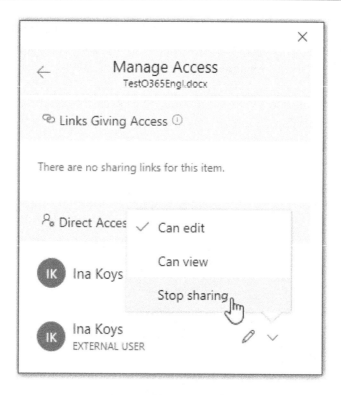

1.4 New and improved general features

Something you may have noticed is the search window, that now is displayed in the centre of the title bar of Office applications.

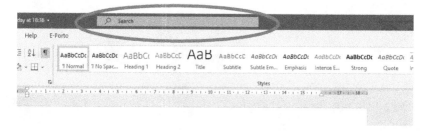

This search window seeks to cover several different search options all in one go. They're getting offered as soon as I click the window.

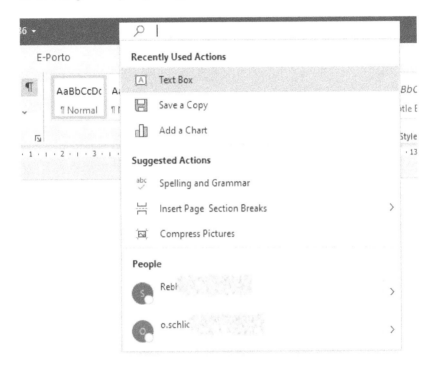

Here, I now can search Microsoft help sites, start certain actions and features or contact people. The suggestions are improved along with the information I write into the search box. Also, documents that seem to fit my search criteria, are getting displayed.

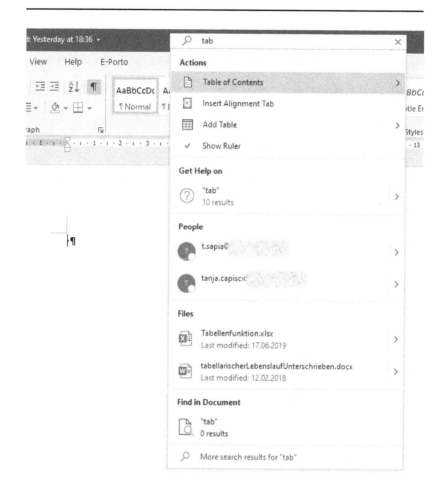

It certainly will be worthwhile simply to check out how this clearly improved search feature can ease one's workload. But indeed, it may simply require too much room. If so, using the **Options**, it can be reduced to a magnifier symbol – pretty much as it can be done in Windows 10 alike. This setting would have to be done in the back-stage area for each of the Office applications separately.

So, if you'd like to reduce room consumption, click **File / Options / General** and select **Collapse the Microsoft Search by default**.

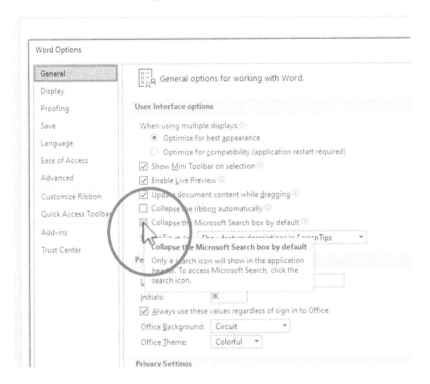

After that, you only get the magnifier symbol, that can be activated on mouse click or **ALT + Q**.

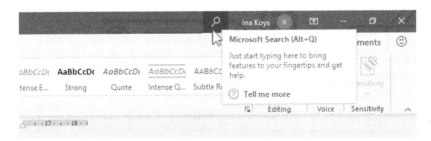

All across the whole Office package there are apart from the storage-related features several other innovations. For instance, there is the **Comments** field next the **Share** button, that for the most part works like it did for a number of versions. But now, they are a bit embellished, so they now also support a thread.

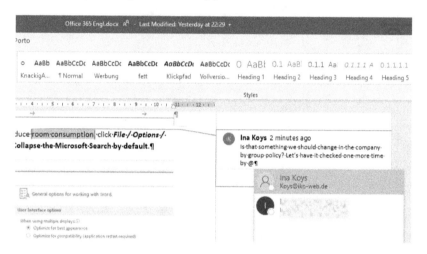

By typing the @ symbol, you can insert people who are automatically getting an email that somebody's referring to them. Also, there is now a way to resolve a thread and to wind up the discussion.

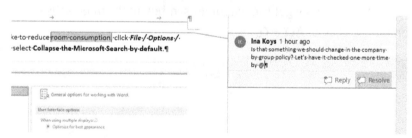

If one wants to delete a comment, it still works i.e. using the right mouse button.

And finally, there is a feature provided using the right mouse button that previously only worked with PowerPoint and now is generally available: the creation of custom external graphics also from tables, shapes and more.

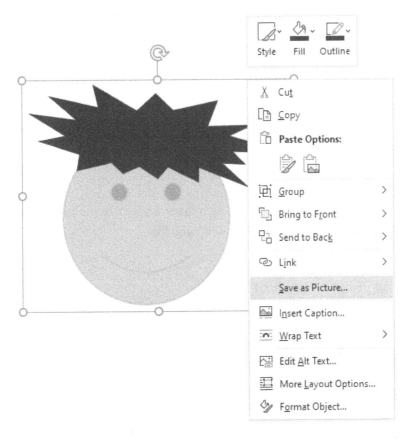

Apart from that, all custom colour dialogues now offer the option to specify a hexadecimal value.

1.5 New entries in the Insert tab

To a large extent, the tab remained as it was. Still, some really nice improvements can be found in the **Illustrations** area. Now, there are several different ways to a much-improved choice of graphics. Let's begin clicking **Pictures** and **Stock Images**.

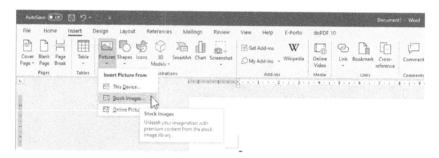

You now get a window with a search feature which in the first place delivers photos. Select or insert what you like.

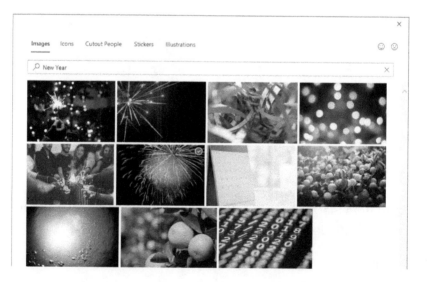

But along with the images, different types are provided like the very popular Icons. All can be found using the search or provided categories. Please note that you may have to scroll left and right through the categories.

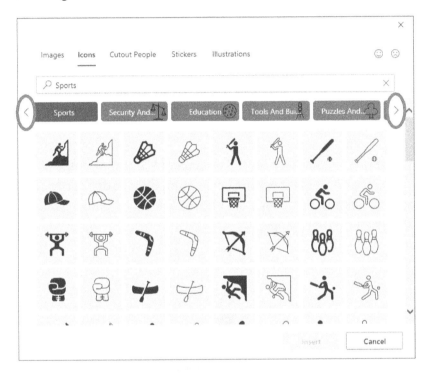

These icons are a major improvement especially for business purposes and will professionalize the look of your graphics.

Using the known graphic formatting features, you can customize the icons to fit your purposes. The choice of icons keeps getting richer and richer, so an occasional look for desired icons may help, if one is not fully happy yet. You also get the Icons using their button in the **Insert** tab.

A really exciting new entry is a feature that at this time is maybe less useful for business purposes than for informal environs like school and study: **3D Models**.

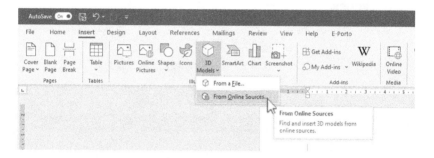

Online one already finds several examples for free download. With them, one can easily check out how to turn them to any desired direction. Some of the models are even animated. Drag them around using their central symbol.

In a standard installation one also finds the **Add-Ins** area near the centre.

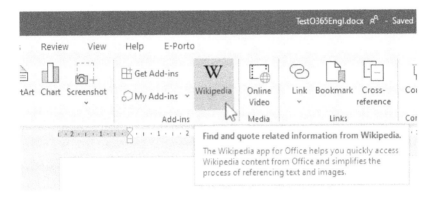

Add-Ins are software snippets of mostly external suppliers, extending the possibilities of an application. A search for information in Wikipedia will certainly be fine. But using many other things you can download from the Microsoft store, be rather conscious. You'd be opening your machine and maybe your company network for the data connections of third parties. If it's only on your private machine, it's your decision. Within companies such an installation will be at least undesired, most likely totally blocked by the IT administration. Therefore, I am not going to talk about this section.

1.6 Draw Tab

For the users of a touchscreen there also is a nice extra: the re-designed **Draw** tab.

In this tab, one can write or draw with a finger on the screen – even though it'll be much more elegant to do so with appropriate pens like Surface pen and others. Here, there one finds a range of different pens and pen properties. Even the simple pen can be used with flashy colours like gold flitter or a starry sky. If one wants to delete drawn sketches again, the eraser will help and maybe a strikethrough of the no more desired parts.

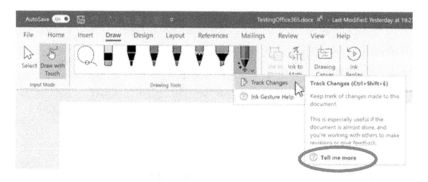

If you use draw functions a lot, you will enjoy adjusting all provided pens and the possibility to highlight a range of drawings using the lasso. The blue **Action Pen** can track changes in your document and edit text with intuitive gestures. For details, click **Tell me more**.

Attempting to draw clear and clean drawings, use **Ink to Shape**. Herewith, more or less orderly sketches will be transformed into geometric shapes. One instantly gets presentable charts!

Generally

For school or scientific purposes clearly more handy than the arduous typing of mathematical formulas is the possibility to write them directly on the screen. It can be processed via **Ink to Math** and then be handled like any other formula.

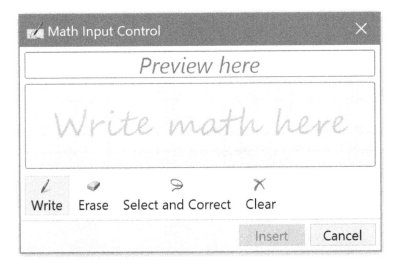

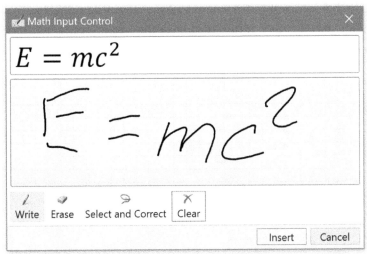

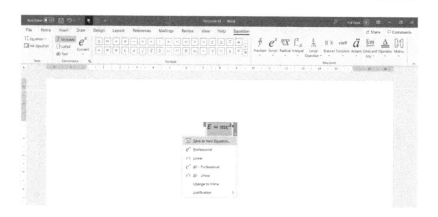

Then, in the far right corner of the **Draw** tab there also is the **Ink Replay** button that lets you draw any entries again on the screen in order of their appearance. That may make sense when recording a screen capture as offered in PowerPoint.

1.7 Picture Format tab

At a first glance, not much seems to have changed on this tab. Still, one now has the new option to change the transparency features of pictures.

Remove Background now omitted the anyway pretty useless frame and instead provides an improved feature of drawing lines to mark the areas to keep and to remove. **Crop** now also allows shapes and if you seek an easier way to submit alternative texts, it now is easier, too, using the **Alt Text** button.

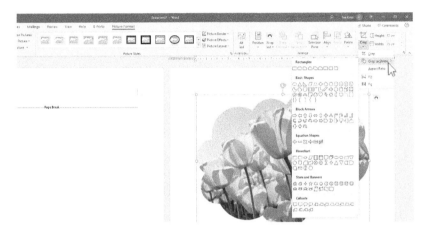

1.8   Help and support

Microsoft understands that the continuous amendment of features and installation of totally new ones is a challenge for the users. Therefore, we have a new tab called **Help**.

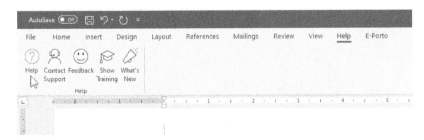

Clicking the **Help** button a new pane opens in order to get browsed.

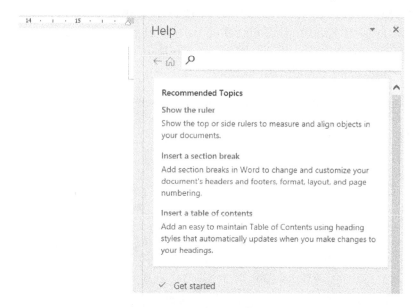

The Help section was completely worked through and definitely deserves a look. Alternatively, you may like to pick a training that often will also contain videos explaining some topics better than simple words could.

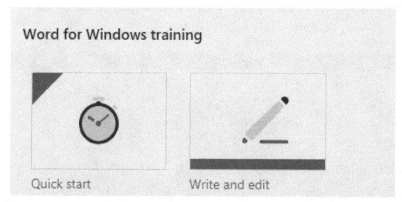

And finally, one can have a look at what happened with the last update and maybe discover new features to polish your documents.

1.9 Backstage area

The **Backstage area** is the part of Office, that opens by clicking **File** on the left of the ribbon. Major changes beyond the ones we already looked at are not applied. But if you start opening an Office app without opening a certain file, you'll find the start area worked through.

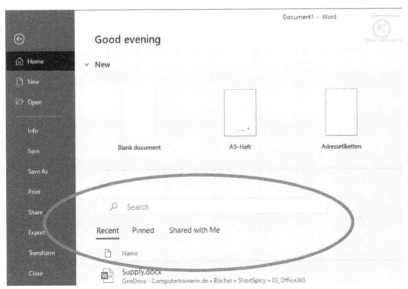

Now, I can easily pick previously used files and also get quick access to documents others shared with me. In a company network, this doesn't even require noticing. The permissions are granted anyway.

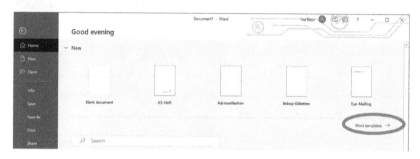

Also, the dazzling selection of templates provided by Microsoft for lots of purposes is not displayed anymore at full scale. Now, I get an array of my pinned templates and below them, my recently used files. Only if I didn't pin any templates yet, I will see the Microsoft suggestions. And if seeking inspiration, I always can click **More templates** to get to the **New** pane known from previous versions.

New is a feature in **Info** that's called **Always Open Read-Only**.

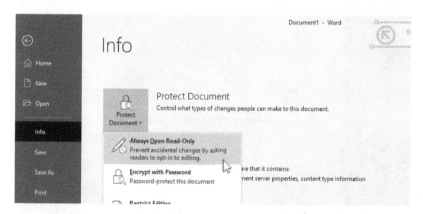

The feature only creates a dialogue similar to the widely ignored **Mark As Final**.

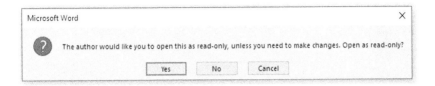

This feature is more a friendly support than a real safety feature. To apply real safety, still the selection of a read-only storage is the method of choice.

From time to time, it will be useful to have a look at one's **Account** to check for updates or to verify the validity of the license that is to be renewed (and payed) every year.

Also, the **Open** dialogue is somewhat renewed. The folders are now shifted into their own tab.

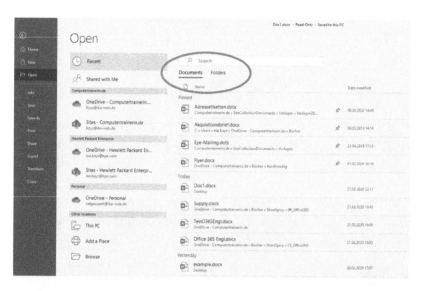

And if other users shared files with me, I'll find them under the respective button even without previous knowledge.

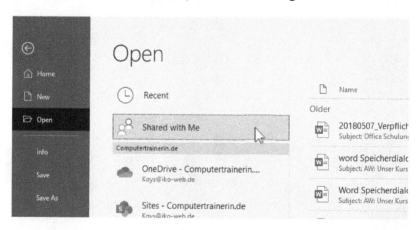

2 Word

The most notable Innovation in Word is probably the **Editor**, displayed on the right of the **Home** tab.

One does not need to click it; it chimes in on its own. It is very ambitioned and provides its opinion regarding style, spelling and punctuation. Yes, it helped me to write this booklet, still, especially in my native language, I would never accept the suggestions without double-checking. It is still a machine and the idea of artificial intelligence remains an idea for another while. The following sequence is correct - according to Editor:

You didn't come on the bus? – Yes, I didn't.

Meanwhile, parts of this booklet are considered bad English.

;round·now·omitted·the·anyway·pretty·useless·frame·
ovides·an·improved·feature·of·c
ep·and·to·remove.·Crop·now·al:
easier·way·to·submit·alternative·texts,·it·now·is·eas-

As you may check, I used the expression anyway. And if you're not sure about your words, you may want to ask the editor explicitly by clicking it. For an example, I now omitted a comma.

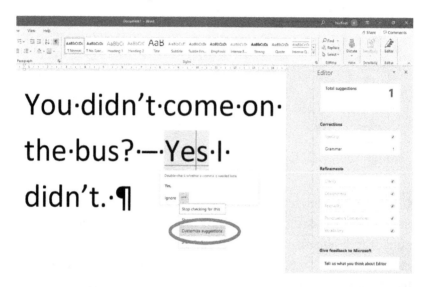

Right-clicking the parts with blue markings, one gets an explanation and next to the **Ignore** entry, three dots to customize the suggestions. To switch them off completely, it'll be quicker to go to *File / Options / Proofing* and to tick off **Check grammar and refinements in the Editor Pane**.

Probably more useful in daily life is the new option to store private copies of cloud documents in one's own OneDrive. These copies are nice to collect one's own ideas regarding a document without instantly making them public. If simply downloading a file, it easily happens that one loses track of what is public and what is not and where exactly a private copy is stored. All of that is now facilitated on the right of the **View** tab under **Create a Private Copy**.

A click creates a copy of the file in a special folder of your personal OneDrive with the file name addition **Private**.

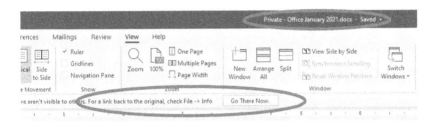

Clicking the **Go There Now** button you'll be directed to the Backstage area where the new folder is presented. And yes, the link to the original file is provided. But finding it is another thing. Microsoft may need to facilitate that the future.

Apart from that, there aren't many new features in Word, but some very interesting ones.

A little change is only found in completely new installations, not in updates of previous Word versions: the list handling is changed now. Now, all previous formatting is kept and only supplied with a bullet point or number. If you want to return to the previous mode, you can do so selecting *File / Options / Advanced / Editing Options / Update style to match selection*.

Then, if you have a microphone in your machine, you now can dictate your texts! It does not take any specific learning, only the activation of the respective service if required. Anyway, keep in mind, that your machine sends the sound files to Microsoft and gets the results returned from there. If you don't like that, abstain from talking with your computer. If you don't mind, just click **Dictate** in the **Home** tab.

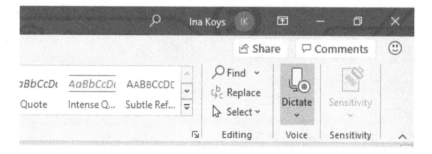

The sentences are first written in small print and sometimes later adjusted. Dictate punctuation along with the text. Formatting is not supported yet, but indeed, if one is not that quick typing, it can already work well. If there seem to be misunderstandings or weird spelling, maybe adjust the language settings.

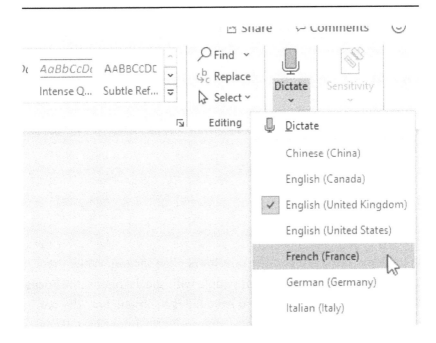

The counterpart of this feature, **Read Aloud**, is hidden in the **Review** tab.

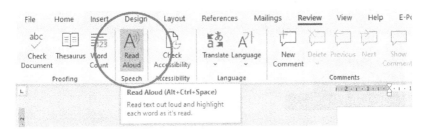

In order to have your text read aloud, it has to be highlighted first. If then a detail does not fit, it can be adjusted using the control bar on the right. I find the voices quite pleasant.

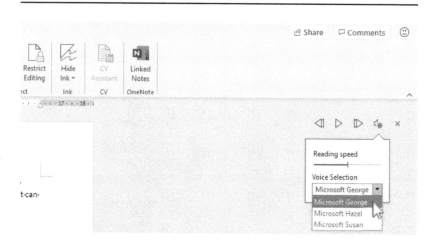

In the **View** tab is are also the new **Immersive** section. While the **Immersive Reader** is meant for people with special needs, the **Focus** switches the screen to dark and even hides the menu bar. The bar returns when moving the mouse pointer to the upper part of the screen and then, can work normally.

You'll get out of the mode by clicking **Focus** again.

3 Excel

In Excel, we now have a whole range of improvements and new features. Very prominent is **Data Analysis**. It is recommended to use **Format as Table** along with it, still, even without it, it works well. I used the table here. The idea is to take questions in normal language. As long as that language is English, go for it.

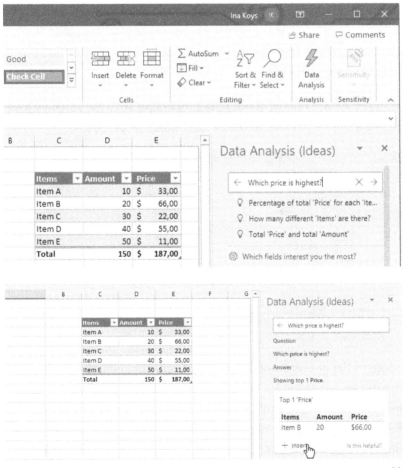

Now clicking **Insert**, you'll get your result on a new sheet.

Alternatively, you may want to check out different charts and pivot tables offered, which may fit for your purposes. At this point, in all languages other than English, these tables are the only option provided by **Data Analysis**.

Now, as we are talking about data processing anyway, you may love the new ability of Excel to read and import PDF values.

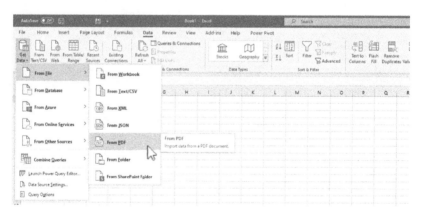

Some of the likewise unobtrusive, but very convenient improvements can easily slip by. One of them is the new possibility to deselect parts of a previously selected range – that did not exist in Excel before. Now, with a previously highlighted range, you can hold down the **CTRL** key and click what you would like to deselect again.

Talking about new entries in **Formulas**, the star certainly is XLOOKUP(). It's the long overdue improvement of the error prone VLOOKUP(). Now, you can search complete areas instead of only the first column and by default, the exact match is returned. If none is found, a custom notification can be specified.

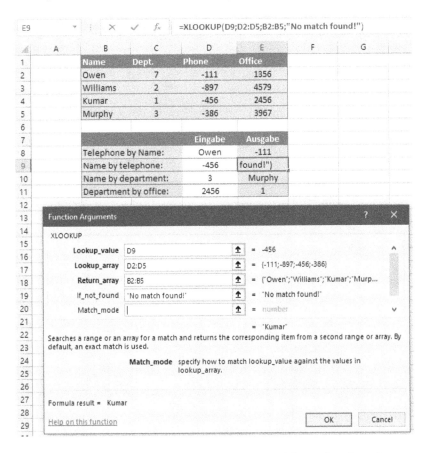

A not instantly visible feature is the support while typing function names. So far, the list was entirely alphabetic. One needed to know the exact name of the function. Now this was improved so as the assistant offers functions with a similar context.

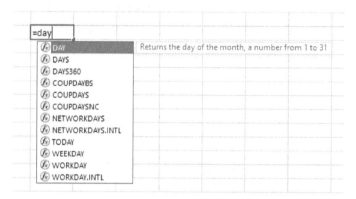

Checking this out, you may already find some of the new functions like CONCAT() and TEXTJOIN(), improving the former CONCATENATE(). As usual, the **Insert Function** wizard (left in the **Formulas** tab) does provide good explanation and examples clicking **Help on this function**.

When searching for data that meet certain conditions, it's worth to have a look at several other new functions like SWITCH(), IFS(), MAXIFS() and MINIFS(). Especially SWITCH() can really facilitate your work when querying various conditions and even provide a default value, if no condition applies.

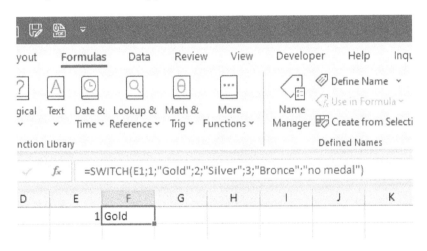

Multi-nested IF()now finally belong to the past!

More new functions can be found checking **Lookup & Reference** in the **Formulas** tab: UNIQUE(), FILTER(), SORT(), SORTBY(). Listing all the functions in the wizard one may also find SEQUENCE(), XMATCH() and RANDARRAY(). For all these functions a built-in help is available as shown.

Another new feature is available for Pivot tables. Pretty often, users preferred a layout other than the one Microsoft supplied by default. Now, all users can fix their preferred layout in the backstage area clicking *File / Options / Data / Data options / Edit default layout*...

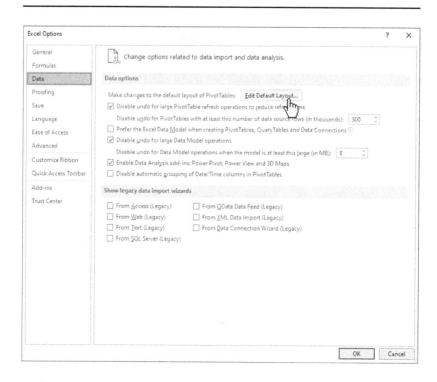

In the next window one can pick one's favoured settings via drop-down. Still, it's even better that one simply can import one's desired settings via mouse click. Click just somewhere into the customized Pivot table and then on **Import**. Everything previously specified is now saved as a default setting for all Pivot tables to come.

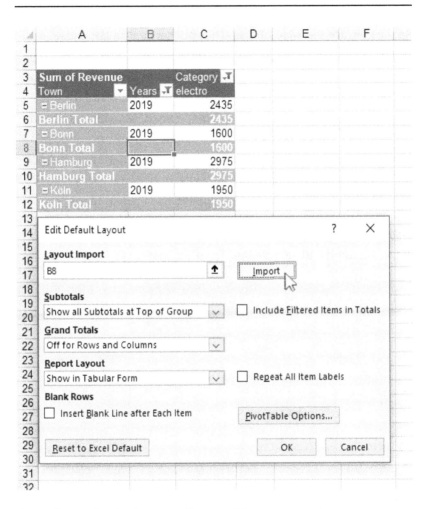

Apart from what is shown so far, great improvements are concerning data visualization. The first new feature to mention is rather simple, it's a new chart type, the **Funnel**. It is meant for the presentation of tapering or piled-up data.

Really new are the **Map Charts**. They are certainly a good idea. And especially regarding geographically relevant data they are only one out of two steps done – and more improvement is announced! But at this time, the feature is still somewhat premature and it's not plain easy to create a perfect example. Indeed, **Map Charts** do not work with cities. Expected are states, countries, regions, or post codes. Sometimes, sorting from larger to smaller units may help Excel to understand the structure. Anyway, it takes an internet connection as the respective data is supplied live by Bing Maps.

Begin highlighting a table or list with regional data in the first and second column and select **Maps** from the **Insert** tab.

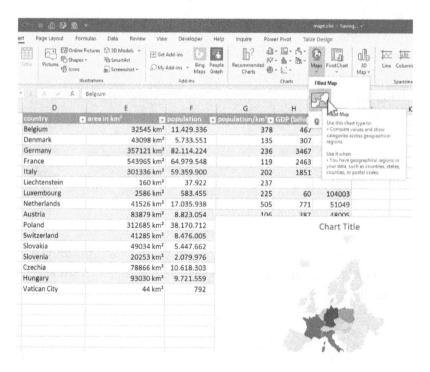

Keep in mind your data is sent to Bing in the background, so stop for a moment to think how sensible the data might be. If you're sure they are alright, just go on. Otherwise, it might be safer to keep off from this indeed convenient visualisation.

The standard design is the way standards are: they normally do well with improvement. To check the offers, I first have a look at the newly displayed context sensitive **Chart Design** tab. Here, I can view several possibilities, but not what I'm looking for: I'd like to have the countries displayed in different colours, rather than in different shades of blue.

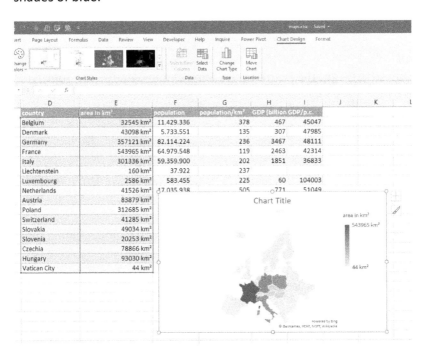

I now first get a map of whole Europe displayed and would like to reduce it to the countries concerned. I right-click somewhere onto the map diagram and select **Format Data Series…**.

Doing that, I get the **Format Data Series** pane, where I can specify that.

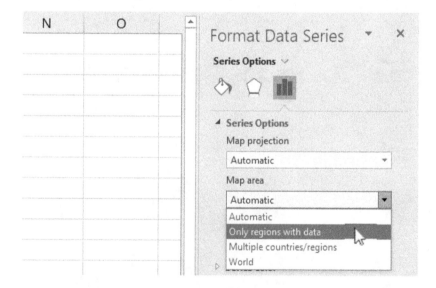

After that, I would like to display the counties not in different shades of blue (or any other colour selected) anymore. This colour refers to the values in the second column, here the area of the different countries. That setting is a bit tricky to find. It can be done i.e., from **Select Data** in the **Chart Design** tab.

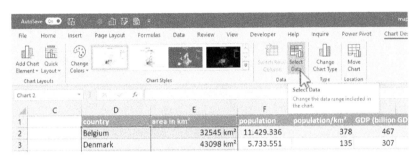

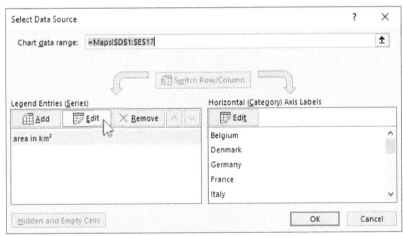

I then get the **Select Data Source** dialogue and now need to edit the legend entries. After adjusting the series values and checking **Color by secondary category names** and clicking **OK** two times everything looks as desired.

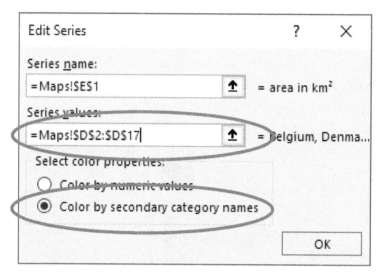

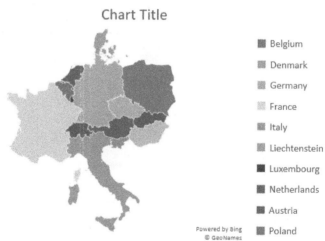

More settings can of course be applied using the tools mentioned.

Maybe that suits for you. But if interested in comprehensive possibilities, you might be better off with **3D Maps**. They haven't really changed since a couple of Excel versions and therefore, are not covered here. The Microsoft help is not very useful here and provides only basic information. With some basic German, you may have a check on my booklet 'Excel auf der Landkarte'. Maybe I'll translate it to English in a while.

Still, these are not the only geographic features now provided by Excel. In the **Data** tab you now find two new data types: **Stocks** and **Geography**. These data types are only available on machines where English is one of the installed Office languages. It is not necessary actually to use English, still, some basic knowledge is helpful. Let's first have a look at the **Geography**. Entries in a local language are understood sometimes and translated. Still, it's better to use the English names.

'**Geography**' is a new data type in Excel and can be handled similar to the object type you may know from programming. It has properties that retrieve statistical information from the internet to supply them simply by mouse click or in calculations. To get it done, suitable text information first needs to be converted to this data type. Many units like settlements, political and geographical units are possible. Still, be aware of confusions with places with the same name. Also, too small places like villages may not be found.

The map symbol indicates the **Geography** data type. If in doubt whether Excel had picked the correct one, click it to retrieve more information. Scroll through the data supplied. All of them can be handled highlighting the cell as properties of your data.

The information one now has within some mouse clicks is abundant and would otherwise require longer research. If you like, you can now simply insert the agricultural land percentage of Italy, the median household income of Iowa, the number of people per household in Berlin, the live expectancy of Greenland or the time zone of Arusha – all within seconds!

Italy		44,0%
Iowa	$	53.183
Berlin		1,83
Greenland		71,8
Arusha		East Africa Time

That can really make your work much easier!

All these entries are written into the next free cell right of your entry. And as already mentioned, this information can be used in equations, formulas, and relations of all kind as it's data property.

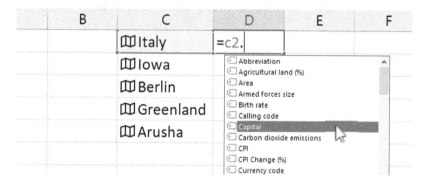

Separated only with a point from the cell reference, the properties can be listed and selected. Working with a list of entries, you can then drag the reference down as usual. If the data type fits, you then get all desired information.

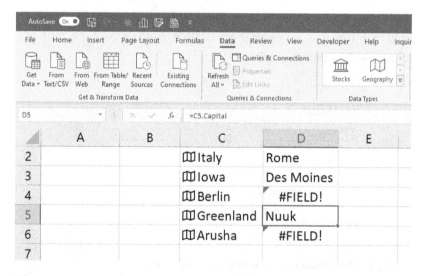

Berlin and Arusha have no capitals. And of course, resulting figures can be used in all kinds of equations.

A	B	C	D
			Number of Women (est.)
		Italy	30275708
		Iowa	1572856
		Berlin	1874074
		Greenland	27996
		Arusha	208221

Alongside the **Geography** data type, you also find the **Stocks** type.

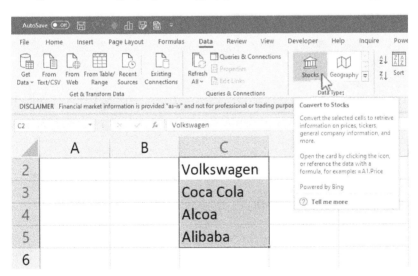

Most of the times, the result will be quite clear, but sometimes, more specifications are required.

Excel

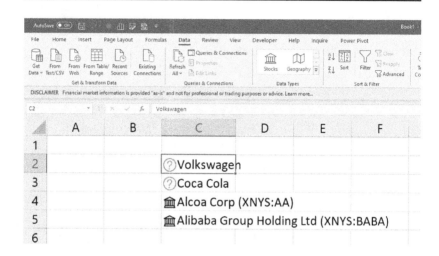

Sometimes, the correction of the company name may help, i.e., with Volkswagen one needs to pick the correct one from the **Data Selector**.

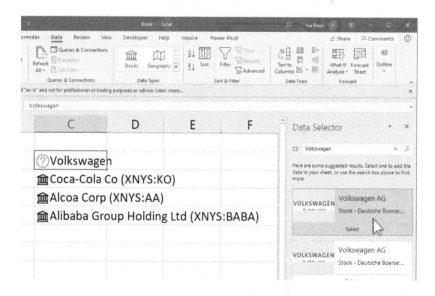

Now, the specific stocks are properly displayed and can be handled as shown for **Geography** data.

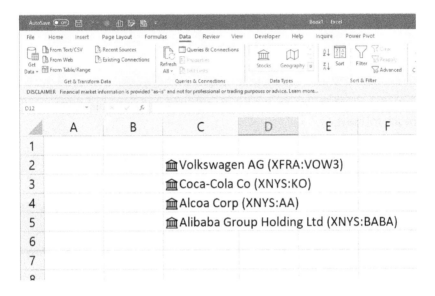

4 PowerPoint

Also in PowerPoint one finds a couple of interesting innovations, some very smart ones also for the users of touchscreens. Let's begin with the features available for any hardware.

First of all, you also can dictate PowerPoint, if you like. Maybe here it makes more sense, as in a good template one does not need much formatting.

Beginning from a blank presentation, you first may find **Design Ideas** on the right.

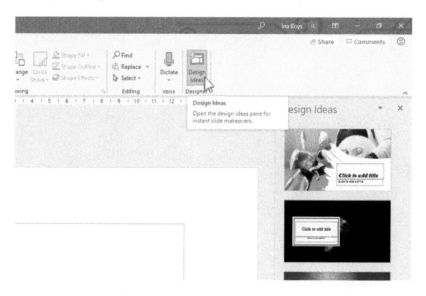

If you intend to create a presentation from scratch, you may find them useful. Still, most companies have their own standard presentation. In this case, simply switch them off using the respective button on the right in the **Home** tab.

A new idea but maybe very worth entering the daily practice is the **Zoom**, to be found in the **Insert** tab.

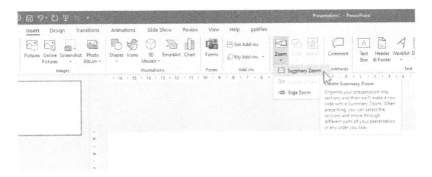

First, let's have a look at the **Summary Zoom**. It creates some kind of optical content slide. First create and finalize all the content you need. Then pick the **Summary Zoom** from the **Insert** tab.

You now get a window to pick your slides from. Activate all slides you'd like to include in your summary zoom and click **Insert**.

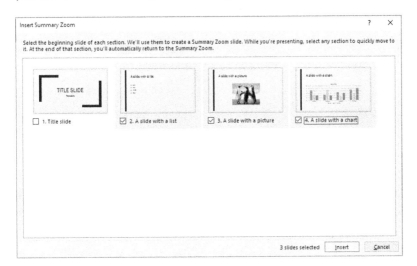

You now get a new slide in your design, that apparently contains your slides as graphics. You only need to add your own title.

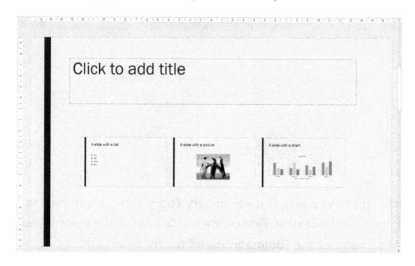

Your new slide looks like it only contains graphics. Still, they only appear in the zoom as you can see clicking one of them. We now have the new context sentive tab **Zoom**. Click to bring it forward.

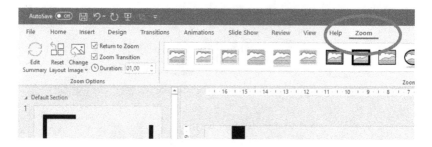

Here, you can apply a number of edits, if you feel like. But first let's have a look at how it works in default mode. To see that, you need to go to **Slide Show** view.

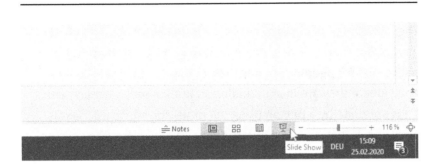

Click the graphics of the different slides. The effect is impressive, but cannot be printed in a book. If some editing is desired, check out the possibilities of the **Zoom** tab.

Alternatively, there are two other types of **Zoom**s. The **Section Zoom** does not refer to single slides, it links to whole sections of slides if you work with them. Here, you first need to add a new slide outside the section and highlight it.

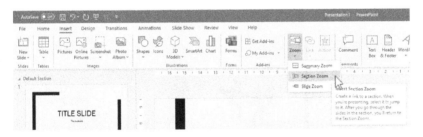

After selecting the section, you get a picture on your slide to dive into that section. At the end of the section, you will return to the slide you came from. A rather flashy effect that - used in a meaningful way - can really make sense. If you don't work with sections, you may want to use the **Slide Zoom** that works using single slides to start from. This zoom does not return to the start slide be default, but can be adjusted accordingly in the **Zoom** tab.

The insertion of pictures does not seem to have changed at first glance. But there is a new detail: you're getting automatically alternative text for people with impaired eyesight. That is certainly a good idea if they are in your audience. But indeed, most presentations are done by a person using the projector. Here, that text is pointless. If that is your standard situation, you can switch off the function under **File / Options / Ease of Access / Automatically generate alt text for me**.

The **Transitions** tab also looks familiar at first. Still, there is a new function that is similar to the **Zoom**, the **Morph**. **Morph** provides soft transitions between the objects on one slide and the next. Herewith it's important to keep in mind it really must be the same objects, not just others looking the same. Therefore, copy the slide with the intended beginning of the **Morph** transitions and paste it in again, i.e. via **CTRL + C** and **CTRL + V**.

Now apply any desired changes in the copied slide. Change size, colours, text, or positions as you like.

Then select for the second and maybe more slides the **Morph** from the **Transitions** tab.

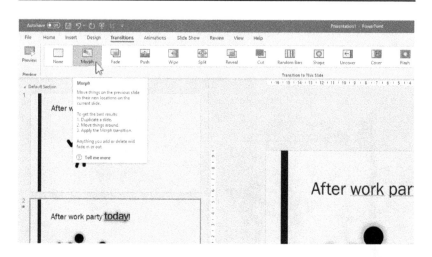

As any transitions will be displayed when coming to a slide, now click the slide you began with and go to **Slide Show** view. Click somewhere and watch the object changing smoothly. If you now intend to apply some changes, you can do so in the **Transitions** tab using **Effect Options**.

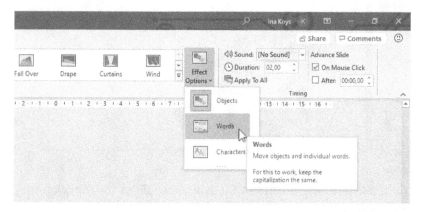

And finally, after the big success of the **Screen Recordings**, there is another feature of that kind: Records of the whole presentation.

Here, one does not simply get a long film file of the presentation. You will have your comments and actions recorded with the corresponding slides. This makes it easy later to re-arrange your presentation without having to begin again from scratch. But it also means that during the transitions from slide to slide nothing is recorded. It also might be a good idea to include a moment of silence at the beginning and end of each slide. And if it appears possible that some users will watch the presentation online, do make sure PowerPoint online supports your transitions.

If you want to record your presentation now, microphone and webcam are recommended, but of course not required. Find the button in the **Slide Show** tab.

Now a new window opens so you can record your comments and maybe drawings on the screen from the beginning or slide by slide. In the bottom part of the screen, you find all buttons and settings. The colour scale is useful if you want to draw on the screen. Two pens, one eraser and 12 colours can be chosen from. In the bottom right corner, you find the picture your webcam is recording. Clicking the symbols underneath you can switch off devices, too. In the upper part of the screen, you find the buttons to start the record, to stop and to replay it.

Pretty useful is the possibility to display your presentation notes while recording. They won't be included in the recording! The buttons on the right will delete the record or allow hardware settings. The arrows left and right of the slide enable you to switch through the presentation. Close the window by hitting **ESC**.

If you want to delete details from a slide, you can do so from the **Slide Show** tab.

In the end, you can go to **File / Export** and store your works in many formats including show, video, GIF or stream.

Sometimes, people feel insecure about their presenting skills. In that case, and currently in English only, you can rehearse with a built-in coach now!

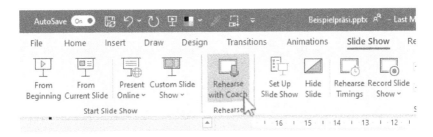

It will open a little window. Switch on your microphone and click **Start Rehearsing**.

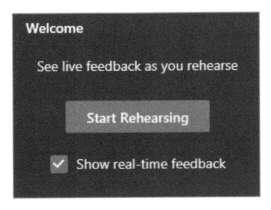

A little window then asks you to start talking. Make your presentation now, nothing will happen before you're finished. After your presentation (or your short version of it), you'll get a report. My demonstration in this case was very short.

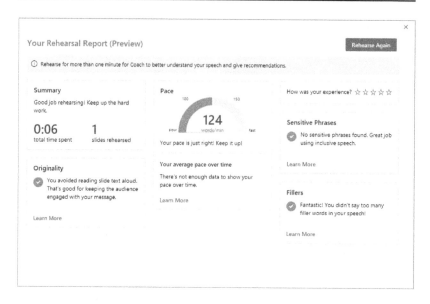

This report will certainly not find every single possible flaw. But it can help you to gain confidence, if needed.

These are features to support you when presenting. There are other features, too, supporting your audience. PowerPoint can provide sub- or overtitles in your presentation. That may appear harmless, but indeed, is a quantum lapse. It is not previously typed text. PowerPoint can display the text simultaneously as you speak or translate to one of the available languages in real time! Find the corresponding settings in the **Slide Show** bar on the right.

The result is pretty exact and in case of need, very worth checking out. Due to my lack of Chinese skills, I tried a translation to French.

> Il s'agit d'un sous-titre traduit par Powerpoint.

A neat sound equipment is certainly a good idea, but even with simple hardware you'll get pretty correct translations. Please be aware the feature is only active in the **Slide Show** view and the texts – translated or recorded - are real time only and not kept.

If you want to switch this feature on or off during the presentation, have an eye on the bottom left corner. There's a toolbar that exists since long but is seldom used. If you don't see it, move your mouse pointer towards it to have it displayed.

Using the three dots on the left, you also can adjust the display of the subtitles during your presentation.

And finally, one feature for the users of tablet computers only: the ruler in the **Draw** tab.

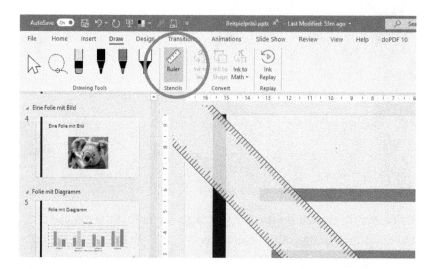

The ruler is displayed now and can be moved parallel across the screen with one finger. Two fingers on the little compass in the middle will twist it to any angle. The ruler can be used to draw straight and orderly lines on the screen with the pen or your finger.

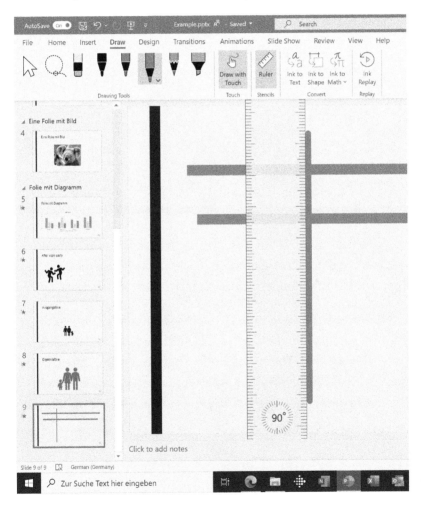

5 Outlook

5.1 View and backstage settings

In Outlook one finds a bunch of small novelties and a change of standards in the ribbon. The tabs are now minimized by default.

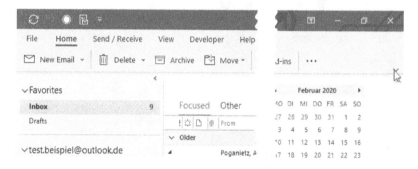

You may have a check, but if you prefer to have all features available, you can unfold the ribbon with the small arrow on the right. Then you get a modernized look, but all the buttons are back.

As all writing features in Outlook are indeed processed by Word, you now can have your email read and dictated, too if your hardware supports that. The corresponding button is in the Outlook window and the mail window, too. Apart from that, you have a filter. It's nice to have, but indeed, it only goes to the well-known search.

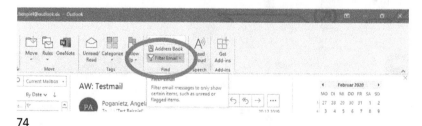

Outlook

Still new is the **Focused** inbox – with the **Other** providing a kind of status between normal mails and spam.

It's certainly a matter of taste. If you don't like it, you can switch it off in the **View** tab and thereby return to the previous version.

For the ones who like to clear their mailboxes quickly, an old tool was brushed up. Using the right mouse button, you can customize the **Quick Actions** now.

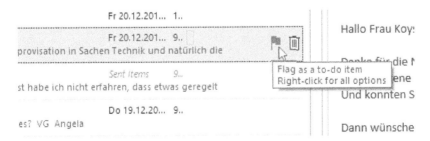

75

In the context menu, you find **Set Quick Actions….** Select it.

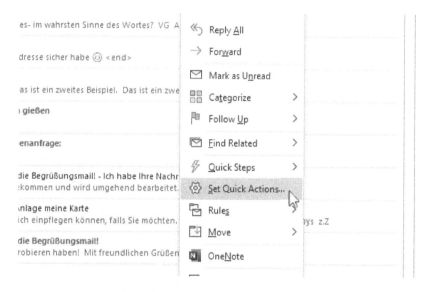

In the now opening dialogue you can pick two more possible actions from the drop-down.

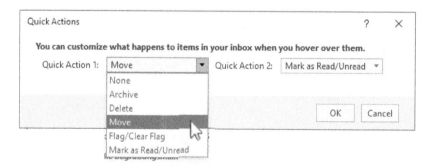

Depending on the selected actions, you will now get two more symbols in the list view when hovering the entries with your mouse pointer.

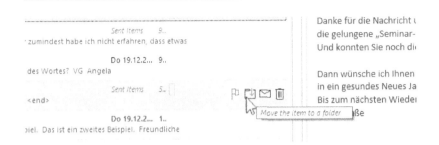

A bunch of well-hidden new features can be found in **Options**. First, you can display a third time zone. Then, after holiday, you may enjoy not to get reminders anymore if the event is over anyway. Or you want to get the reminder always in the foreground, above all other windows. You can now specify this in **Options** now.

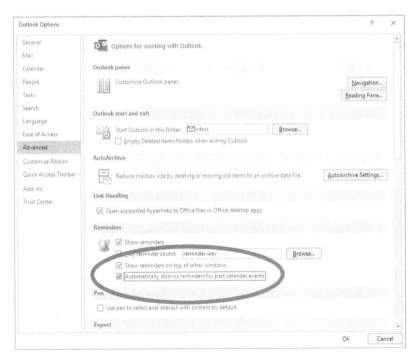

And if you keep forgetting a buffer between your appointments, now Outlook can do that for you.

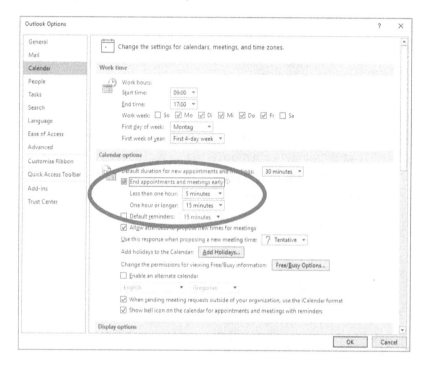

In Outlook, finding missed items is very important. The possibilities provided were always somewhere between alright and really good. Still, people often didn't find them at all or only the basic features and adjustments. Microsoft now offers a different way again that is easy to find and nearly self-explanatory. Starting from the search in the title bar, users can type in any text and thus, start a normal search. But under the little arrow on the right of the search input field, Outlook-specific criteria can be defined to refine the results.

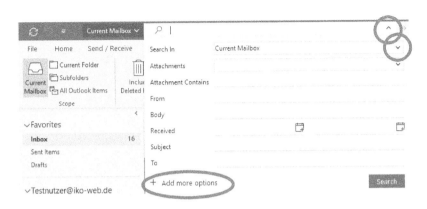

The search remembers your previous search range. The mailbox will include all content but may take long. So start by specifying a certain folder, maybe including subfolders. Please note you can even search for the content of attachments! And if still no avail - or too much! - click **Add more options** to get to the previous **Search** bar and more advanced settings.

5.2 E-Mail

Here, we have a long overdue improvement for all users who intend to use repetitive text snippets in their mails. The use of mail templates wasn't funny anymore since a number of program versions. You now can forget about it in total: you have something better. Most of the times, you won't even need the **Quick Parts** anymore – if you know them at all. Now, you have templates to use within any email window. You can switch the **Template** area on or off as you like using the button on the right.

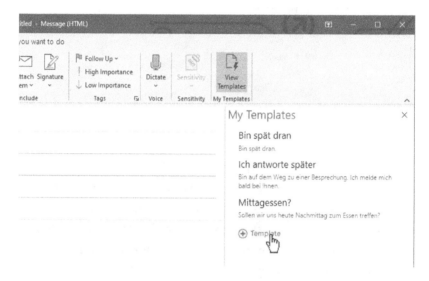

Here, you get some suggestions provided by Microsoft. You can use or delete them. Clicking **Template** you can add your own text templates.

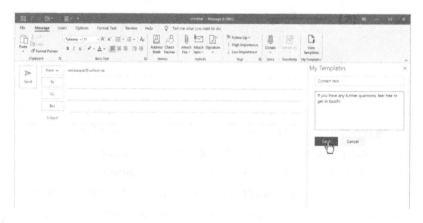

The text snippets are lined up on the right and can be used on any position of the email.

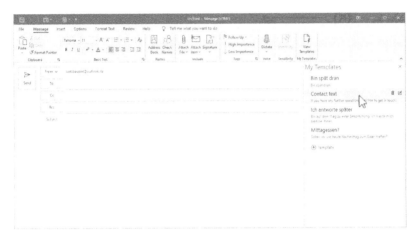

Maybe you know that Outlook doesn't write your mails - Word does. Therefore, you now have the Editor in here, too, with the settings you may have adjusted in Word. If you want to switch it off, do so clicking **File / Options / Mail / Spelling and Autocorrect ...** and uncheck **Check grammar and refinements in the Editor Pane**.

A new entry from extern is a feature you may know from different apps and normal personal use: the **@-mentions**. Of course, you can write the @ in the text of an email, simply to address one person out of a number of recipients. But there is more function provided.

Think of an email that is addressed to a bunch of readers. Then, the writer remembers that one specific item is meant for somebody specific not yet included in the list of recipients. By writing the @ in the mail text, Outlook will make suggestions whom to address.

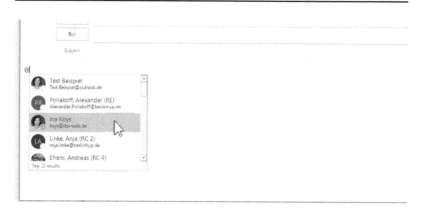

You can simply pick the person from the list or type in somebody else. Indeed, you can work like this with the @ in any Office 365 application now, but here, it suits the context.

After that, two things happen at once. First: the formatting of the specific recipient is different. Then, the email of this person is silently added in the **To:** field.

Now, it might be easier to keep one's train of train of thought. In some environments, along with the **All / Unread** or **Focused / Other** one has another tab **Mentions**. This will then be the place to find the messages received via this feature. If you do not have a **Mentions** tab, you can anyway filter by this feature.

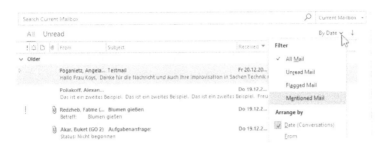

Maybe you know the voting buttons that were nice some versions ago, and then became pretty invisible and therefore, pointless. Now we have something much better: **Poll**, to be found in the **Insert** tab.

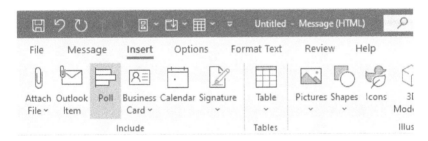

In the pane opening by clicking **Poll**, you can put your question, at least two answer options and decide whether you want to allow multiple answers. After clicking **Insert poll into email**, you'll be inserted as cc recipient, too. In that received copy, you can answer the questions yourself and view the results.

The feature is powered by **Forms**, which provides many more features. If you have a whole questionnaire, rather use **Forms** as a stand-alone. **Polls** is only for a short and quick survey.

Outlook

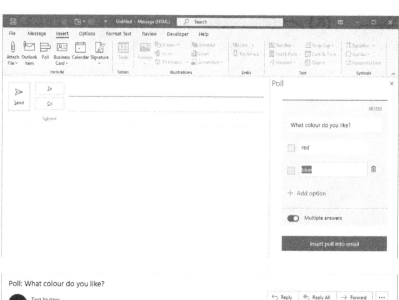

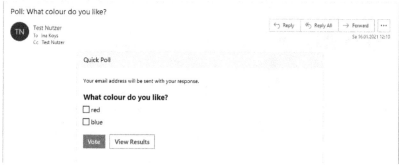

If you correspond in different languages, you now can get a translation with a mouse click.

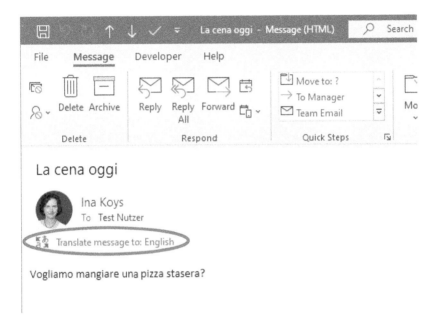

And finally: If you enjoy animated *.gif graphics in emails, you now can use them here, too. Do make sure your mail is HTML formatted.

5.3   Calendar

Some details are improved here, too. When creating a new appointment, we now get suggestions in the **Location** field. This could be from the rooms listed in your company directory, from your previously chosen locations or a simple inspiration by Bing Maps. These suggestions are improved as you write.

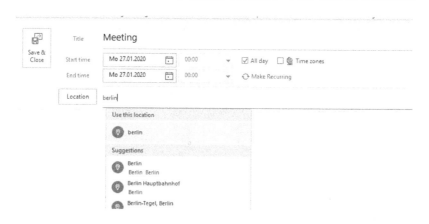

If you now add participants to the meeting, you will get suggestions from the company directory and your contacts, too.

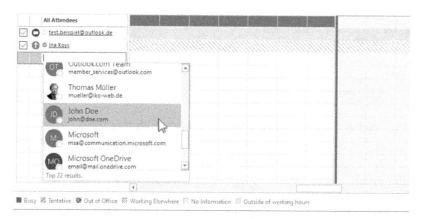

If your company provides the room reservation via Outlook, you now can also reserve several rooms, if you need to do so.

Another long-awaited feature is the feedback of invitations. Now, it's not only the meeting organizer anymore who can view the reactions. Now, every attendant can do so directly in the appointment.

5.4 Groups

Groups are a fairly new feature – not only in Outlook, across the whole Office 365, too. It's an interesting concept as the members of a group don't get only the new messages as they do in a Contact Group. A **Group** keeps all messages for all members, even if they change over time. A new member doesn't need much time to settle into the matter – just add him or her to the group and the whole development of a topic is open for information. Accordingly, people leaving the group won't be bothered anymore.

Groups are supported by different Office365 applications and work all the same once created. Here, we'll only have a look at the ones created within Outlook. By default, this new **Groups** feature can be used by everyone. But in some cases, the administrator may switch the feature off. Normally, you'll find it on the right of the **Home** tab.

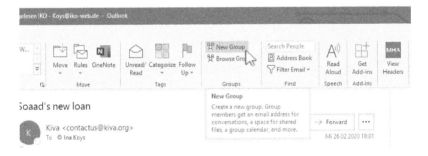

All **Groups** have their own email to be contacted. Within the company, this email can be viewed and contacted by everyone. The access for external organizations can be allowed later when editing the already existing group.

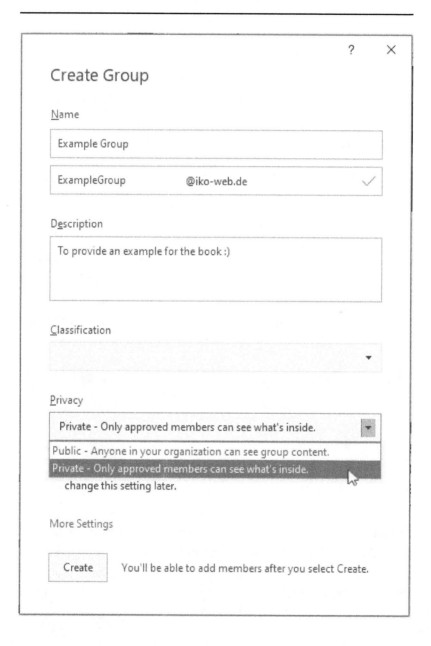

Generally, there are two types of groups: Public and private ones. Anyone can join a public group at will. If the group is made private, one needs permission to join and view the content. All **Groups** can include external members in order to streamline the communication. After clicking **Create** one finds the new group in the bottom part of the **Navigation** pane.

This group already received an email explaining the functionality.

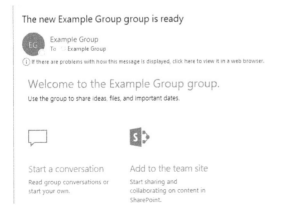

If you later want to apply different settings, click the Group name in the **Navigation** pane to get the **Groups** bar displayed. Editing the group, you can i.e., review your settings, ad a picture or delete the group, if no longer required.

As **Groups** is a cloud feature, clicking the **Edit** in graphic symbol opens Outlook Online, where a picture can be picked using the pen symbol.

The new picture is used to display the group in Outlook, even though it may take a moment to update the information.

Once the **Groups** group is set up, emails can be sent to the group address and remain accessible for all members until the whole group is deleted.

The members receive new messages by default in their inbox or alternatively only in the group folder, according to the group settings. And as a side effect, the new **Groups** also bring back the often-missed group calendars.

5.5 Insights and MyAnalytics

Just like a modern assistant doesn't have much in common with the secretary of bygone days anymore, also Outlook changes from a simple email editor to an all-encompassing support in all aspects of life. As one part of that, you now get automatic reports, how – as far as Outlook is informed – you spent your time last week. This information is targeted entirely for the user and maybe helps indeed to prioritize your day.

If you'd like to get more than status reports, check out the Insights symbol on the right of your Outlook **Home** tab and several other Outlook screens. Using the **Gear symbol** you can apply adjustments.

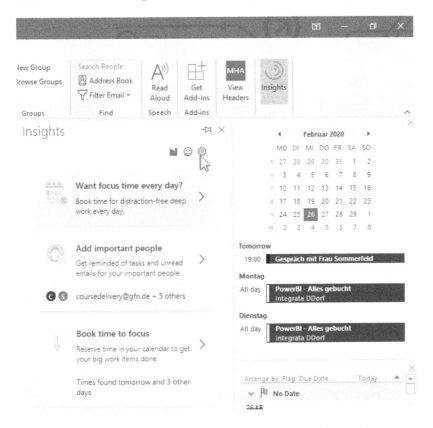

If you then click the **Chart symbol** in the you'll get redirected to a website within your Office365 account providing many more statistics and visualizations.

And maybe indeed this of course limited statement can help to adjust your priorities in line with your intensions.

6 More

The **Short & Spicy** series is available for the most part as e-book and print through many distributors. The volumes 1 and 2 are Amazon exclusive.

Vol. 1:   Outlook as your personal assistant (Outlook 2010-2016)
Vol. 2:   Office 2019 – what's new?
Vol. 3:   Office 365 – What's new?
Vol. 4:   The Digital Notebook
Vol. 5:   Outlook 365 As Your Personal Assistant
Vol. 6:   How to Create Explainer Videos
Vol. 7:   Roll away the boring stuff!

Find these and all new ones clicking
www.shortandspicy.online